CITIES OF THE WORLD

NEW ORLEANS

BY G. S. PRENTZAS

CHILDREN'S PRESS®
A Division of Grolier Publishing
New York London Hong Kong Sydney
Danbury, Connecticut

CONSULTANT

Linda Cornwell
Learning Resource Consultant
Indiana Department of Education

Project Editor: Downing Publishing Services
Design Director: Karen Kohn & Associates, Ltd.
Photo Researcher: Jan Izzo
Pronunciations: Courtesy of Tony Breed, M.A., Linguistics, University of Chicago

---

NOTES ON FRENCH PRONUNCIATION

The words in this book are pronounced basically the way the pronunciation guides look. There are a few notes, however: *ah* is like a in father; *a* is as in can; *ar* is as in far; *ai* and *ay* are like *ai* in rain; *aw* is as in draw; *oh*, *oa*, and *oe* are like *o* in rope; *ow* and *aow* are always as in cow, never as in tow; *u* and *uh* are very short and quick, like *a* in about; *igh* and *ie* are like *igh* in light. Some sounds in French do not occur in English. Notice how you hold your lips to say "oo," and then notice where you put your tongue to say "ee"; now, to pronounce *ew*, hold your lips to say "oo" but move your tongue forward to say "ee." To say *ooh* is similar; say "ooh" as in book, but move your tongue forward to say "ay."

Library of Congress Cataloging-in-Publication Data
Prentzas, G. S.
New Orleans / by G. S. Prentzas.
p. cm. — (Cities of the world)
Includes bibliographical references and index.
Summary: Describes the history, culture, daily life, food, people, sports, and points of interest in the largest city in Louisiana.
ISBN 0-516-20788-1 (lib.bdg.)   0-516-26397-8 (pbk.)
1. New Orleans (La.)—Juvenile literature.   [1. New Orleans (La.)]
I. Title.   II. Series: Cities of the world (New York, N.Y.)
F379.N54P74   1998   98-22247
976.3'35—dc21   CIP
                                                  AC

TABLE OF CONTENTS

LET THE GOOD TIMES ROLL!   *page 5*

NOLA   *page 13*

BEAUTIFUL CRESCENT IN THE RIVER   *page 27*

THE RHYTHM OF THE CITY   *page 45*

A MODERN CITY   *page 53*

FAMOUS LANDMARKS   *page 56*

FAST FACTS   *page 58*

MAP OF NEW ORLEANS   *page 60*

GLOSSARY   *page 61*

PHOTO CREDITS   *page 62*

INDEX   *page 63*

TO FIND OUT MORE   *page 64*

ABOUT THE AUTHOR   *page 64*

ROLL!

ew Orleanians know how to have a good time. Whether it's joining the boisterous crowds at a Mardi Gras parade, dancing to a lively Cajun tune at the Jazz and Heritage Festival, watching alligators at the Audubon Zoo, cruising the Mississippi River on a paddle-wheel steamboat, cheering the NFL Saints at the Louisiana Superdome, or feasting on such local specialties as gumbo, crawfish, or po' boys, there's always something fun to do. Unlike most North American cities, New Orleans is full of music, parades, and good times year-round, reaching its high point with the annual Mardi Gras festivities.

Mardi Gras (MAHR-DEE-GRAW)
Cajun (KAY-JUNN)

MARDI GRAS

Left: A feathered Mardi Gras mask
Above: Costumed participants in a Mardi Gras parade

Most people associate New Orleans with Mardi Gras, the colorful annual event in which more than a million revelers jam the city's streets for several days of parading and merrymaking. Mardi Gras (a French phrase meaning "Fat Tuesday") is held on the Tuesday before Ash Wednesday—the first day of Lent, the forty-day period observed by Roman Catholics and other Christians as a period of penance and fasting. This means that Mardi Gras is always observed in February or early March, depending on when Easter falls. Mardi Gras was first celebrated in Louisiana by French colonists in the early eighteenth century. Today, it is a legal holiday in New Orleans, and the festivities bring millions of dollars into the local economy.

Mardi Gras, also known as Carnival, is celebrated in many places around the world, but nowhere is the festival more spectacular than in New Orleans. The city's

Mardi Gras celebrations are called the "greatest free show on Earth," but many New Orleanians leave town to avoid the mobs of tourists and the disruption of the city's life. Although some festivities are now held before Christmas, the Mardi Gras season officially begins on January 6 with a series of parties and balls. Over the weeks leading up to Mardi Gras day, New Orleans vibrates with parades, music, and dancing. Various krewes, or carnival clubs, sponsor more than fifty parades and about seventy masked balls during the Mardi Gras season. Most of these balls are strictly private, by-invitation-only affairs. (On Lundi Gras, the day before Mardi Gras, crowds flock to a free, public masked ball held at Spanish Plaza.)

A ten-year-old girl riding on a Mardi Gras parade float wears a blue costume and blue face paint.

krewe (KROO)
Lundi Gras (LUN-dee GRAW)

7

The fun is in full swing when the street parades begin. Each parade is organized and paid for by a specific krewe. The parades of Comus, Rex, Bacchus, Orpheus, and the Zulu Social Aid and Pleasure Club are among the most popular. Marching bands and floats wind their way through the streets as thousands crowd the parade route. Dressed in vivid costumes or masks, float riders toss "throws"—candy, colored plastic beads, doubloons (mock Spanish coins made of aluminum or plastic), and other trinkets—into the throngs. Eager spectators try to attract their attention by yelling, "Throw me something, Mister!" The Zulu krewe even gives coconuts to a few lucky bystanders along its parade route. Many of the floats and marchers in the parades are festooned in the traditional Mardi Gras colors—purple (for royalty), gold (for wealth), and green (for faith).

Below: An elaborate and vividly colored float in a Mardi Gras parade
Right and opposite page: Doubloons and beads such as those thrown to the crowd by riders on floats

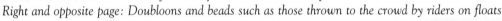

Mardi Gras day in New Orleans is simply one giant party. At about sunrise, paraders in costume and trucks pulling floats begin gathering at parade starting points. All over the city, Mardi Gras Indians, decked out in their colorful costumes, and various marching clubs begin wandering through the city. Loosely organized groups of people dressed up in a wide range of elaborate, funky, or silly costumes also roam the city, making their own fun. The Zulu Krewe, whose members are mostly African-American, is in charge of the first official parade of the day. Costumed in grass skirts and carrying spears, the Zulus march down Canal Street in the morning. In the afternoon, the Rex parade takes center stage. Leading the Rex parade is the King of Carnival, a local resident rewarded for his civic leadership. Next up are the Krewe of Elks and the Krewe of Orleanians. These two popular parades consist of long processions of trucks, each pulling a float. These two parades provide spectators with the best chance to catch a "throw." The festivities continue after sunset, but at the stroke of midnight, Mardi Gras officially ends. Police quickly clear the streets, and street cleaners begin collecting the mounds of garbage left behind by the merrymakers.

Mardi Gras Indians

Mardi Gras Indians are African-American groups that participate in Mardi Gras festivities. They make their own flamboyant costumes, which are colorful combinations of feathers, beads, and sequins. Mardi Gras Indians sing, dance, and play music as they march along the city's streets. There are about a dozen "tribes" in existence, including the Wild Magnolias (left), the Golden Eagles, and the Guardians of the Flame.

OTHER CELEBRATIONS

Mardi Gras isn't the only celebration in town. Throughout the year, there's always some sort of festival or parade going on. Held each spring in late April through early May, the New Orleans Jazz and Heritage Festival attracts large crowds. During the day, people flock to various heritage fairs, which feature regional music, food booths, and traditional crafts. Nighttime concerts around the city present many types of music: jazz, blues, gospel, Cajun, zydeco, country and western, and almost everything else. Jazz Fest showcases such superstars as James Brown and Herbie Hancock, as well as such local favorites as Alvin "Red" Tyler and the Radiators.

On St. Patrick's Day, thousands of green-clad revelers turn out for a fun-filled parade in tribute to New Orleans's large Irish population. Two days later, on March 19, the city's Italian community celebrates St. Joseph's Day by building altars laden with fresh fruits, vegetables, and pastries. African-Americans celebrate during the week-long Black Heritage Festival. These festivals and traditions are among the many in New Orleans that are deeply rooted in the city's colorful history and its diverse cultural and ethnic heritage.

Above: A Mardi Gras Indian performing a chant at the Jazz and Heritage Festival

Left: A Mardi Gras mask

Fun City

A popular Cajun phrase sums up the spirit of New Orleans: *Laissez les bon temps rouler!* (French for "Let the good times roll!")

Above: A Mardi Gras mask
Left: Ray Charles performing at the New Orleans Jazz and Heritage Festival

Laissez les bon temps rouler!
(LESS-AY LAY BAWN TAWNCE ROO-LAY)

11

ew Orleans charms both residents and visitors because it is unlike any other city in the world. Its rich cultural heritage—French, Spanish, African, American, Irish, Italian, German, Hispanic, and Caribbean, among others—gives it a refined yet exotic ambiance. Visitors to the city often say they feel as if they're in Europe or South America instead of the United States. A subtropical climate, a leisurely pace, and friendly residents make it an ideal place to experience an incredible variety of sights, sounds, and tastes. New Orleans is known throughout the world for its diverse culture, elegant architecture, and refined cuisine.

AROUND TOWN

The most famous neighborhood in New Orleans is the French Quarter, or Vieux Carré (French for "Old Square"). The 86-square-block French Quarter is a National Historic District, and its quaint, narrow streets recall bygone times. Many of the eighteenth- and nineteenth-century buildings and town houses have balconies decorated with delicate wrought iron. Delightful little cottages accented with gables and French windows also dot the Quarter. Private inner courtyards burst with jasmine, banana and fig trees, flowers, and herbs. More than 5,000 people live in the French Quarter, and its shops, restaurants, music clubs, and other businesses attract thousands of tourists each day. Reflecting its diverse heritage, the street signs in the French Quarter are in French, Spanish, and English.

Jackson Square sits at the heart of the French Quarter. It is a favorite place for musicians, clowns, mimes, tap dancers, magicians,

Vieux Carré (VYOOH KAH-RAY) *mirliton* (MEER-LEH-TONE) *chayote* (CHIGH-YOE-TEE) *beignet* (BEN-YAY)

A carriage in Jackson Square

Where Am I?

There's no one right way to pronounce "New Orleans." Locals say "NAW-lins," "NYAW-lins," or "NOR-lyuns." Only visitors refer to the city as "Noo Or-LEENS" or "Noo OR-luns." Today, many people just say "NOLA," short for New Orleans, LA.

New Orleans French Market

fortune-tellers, and other entertainers to perform. Clustered around the square are the St. Louis Cathedral, the Cabildo, and several museums. The Cabildo, once the center of government under Spanish rule, houses local historical documents and exhibits. The imposing bronze statue of Andrew Jackson, sitting astride his horse, rises up in the middle of Jackson Square.

The French Market stretches along Decatur and North Peters streets. It features many shops and a market offering fresh seafood and produce, including such local favorites as Creole tomatoes, mirlitons (squash-like pears, also known as chayote), pecans, and watermelons. Locals and visitors enjoy sitting at the tables at one of the French Market's coffeeshops. Over a glass of cold milk or a cup of New Orleans's famous chicory-flavored coffee and a basket of beignets, tasty square doughnuts covered with powdered sugar, they chat and watch the world go by.

Above: A French Market sign
Left: A vendor selling garlic and squash in the French Market

The Central Business District, CBD for short, offers a stark contrast to the French Quarter. The graceful old commercial buildings now stand alongside new hotels, a modern shopping mall called Riverwalk, and such towering skyscrapers as the 51-story Number One Shell Square. Also located in the CBD are the Louisiana Superdome, the Ernest N. Morial Convention Center, and the Civic Center, which houses the city and parish (county) government offices.

A mansion in the Garden District

Streetcars

One of the most popular attractions in New Orleans, for visitors and townsfolk alike, is the St. Charles Streetcar line. Begun as a mule-and-carriage line in 1835, it is one of the world's oldest street railway systems. Today, the old-fashioned green cars, with their wooden seats and plank floors, start in the Central Business District, clatter down St. Charles Street through the Garden District, and turn around at Palmer Park for the return trip. The red streetcars of the modern Riverfront Streetcar line run along the riverfront from the French Market to the Convention Center.

The Garden District, in the city's uptown area, is famous for its beautiful old mansions. This is the city's wealthiest residential section, home to many long-time New Orleans families. Many of the mansions have wonderful grounds and gardens.

The Audubon Zoo is located in the Garden District. The zoo is home to about 1,800 animals that live in simulated natural habitats, such as the special Louisiana swamp exhibit.

Other New Orleans neighborhoods include the Warehouse District—now known for its art galleries, trendy restaurants, and hip clubs—and the mostly residential neighborhoods of Faubourg Marigny, Carollton, Lakeview, and Gentilly.

Children may ride camels at the Audubon Zoo.

Toy crocodiles like this one are souvenirs of the Audubon Zoo.

Faubourg Marigny (FOE-BERG MARE-IN-EE)

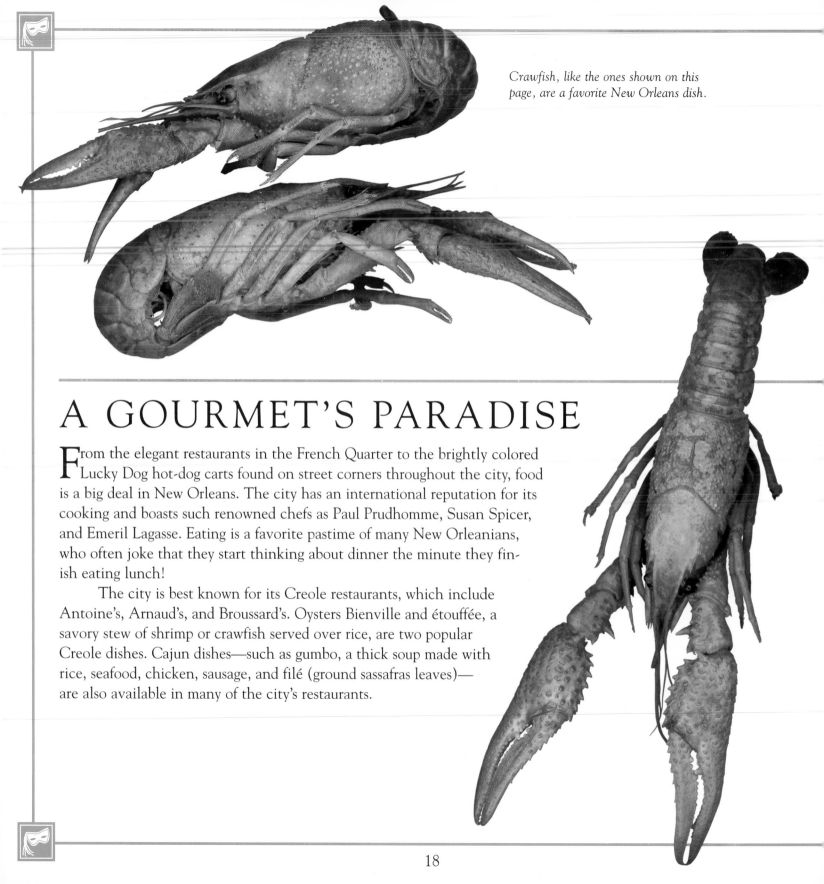

Crawfish, like the ones shown on this page, are a favorite New Orleans dish.

A GOURMET'S PARADISE

From the elegant restaurants in the French Quarter to the brightly colored Lucky Dog hot-dog carts found on street corners throughout the city, food is a big deal in New Orleans. The city has an international reputation for its cooking and boasts such renowned chefs as Paul Prudhomme, Susan Spicer, and Emeril Lagasse. Eating is a favorite pastime of many New Orleanians, who often joke that they start thinking about dinner the minute they finish eating lunch!

The city is best known for its Creole restaurants, which include Antoine's, Arnaud's, and Broussard's. Oysters Bienville and étouffée, a savory stew of shrimp or crawfish served over rice, are two popular Creole dishes. Cajun dishes—such as gumbo, a thick soup made with rice, seafood, chicken, sausage, and filé (ground sassafras leaves)—are also available in many of the city's restaurants.

Antoine's (AN-TWAHNS)
Arnaud's (ARE-NOSE)
Broussard's (BROO-sards)
étouffée (AY-TOO-FAY)
Creole (KREE-ole)
filé (FEE-LAY)

Right: Chef Austin Lishe of Chez Helene
with a customer
Below left: A boy holds a plate of boiled
crawfish.
Below right: A waiter shows off a selection
of typical New Orleans food.

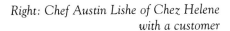

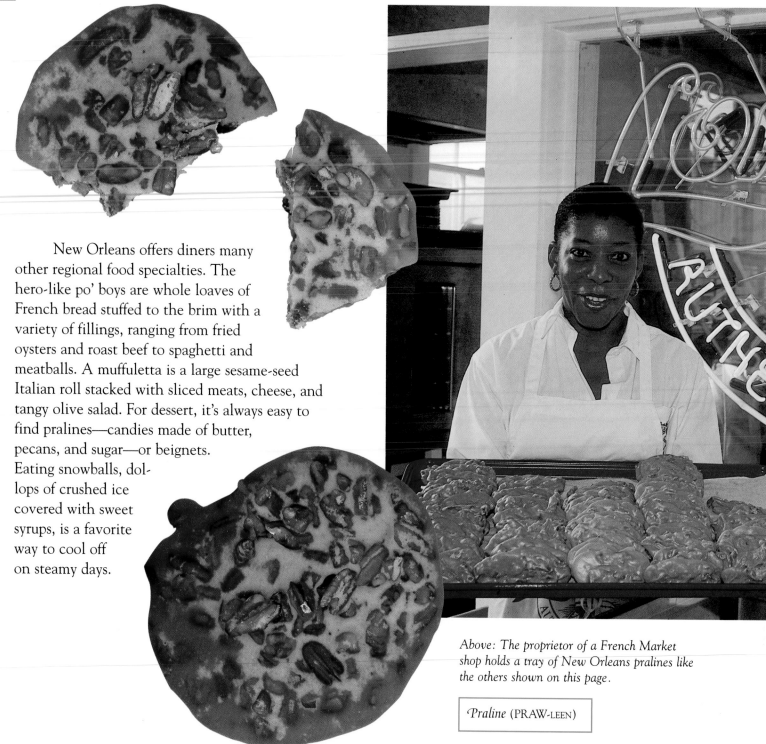

New Orleans offers diners many other regional food specialties. The hero-like po' boys are whole loaves of French bread stuffed to the brim with a variety of fillings, ranging from fried oysters and roast beef to spaghetti and meatballs. A muffuletta is a large sesame-seed Italian roll stacked with sliced meats, cheese, and tangy olive salad. For dessert, it's always easy to find pralines—candies made of butter, pecans, and sugar—or beignets. Eating snowballs, dollops of crushed ice covered with sweet syrups, is a favorite way to cool off on steamy days.

Above: The proprietor of a French Market shop holds a tray of New Orleans pralines like the others shown on this page.

Praline (PRAW-LEEN)

Creole and Cajun

The two words most often associated with New Orleans cooking are Creole and Cajun. Creole generally refers to the descendants of those families, primarily French and Spanish, that settled in New Orleans before the Louisiana Purchase (1803). The term Creole originally meant "native of the colony," but today the word means different things to different people. Creole cooking was perfected in the kitchens of New Orleans. With its rich sauces and many spices, it is elegant and citified.

Cajun is a term coined by early American settlers in Louisiana. It refers to the French-speaking settlers—Acadians—who were forced to leave Canada in the mid-1700s. Most Acadians settled in rural Louisiana along the bayous. Although it developed in the rural areas outside of New Orleans, spicy Cajun cooking is popular in the city.

A restaurant owner in a white lace dress holds a plate of Cajun food.

Marie Laveau (MAH-REE LAH-VOE)

CITIES OF THE DEAD

Among the most unusual sights in New Orleans are its cemeteries. Because most of the city is below sea level, New Orleanians have to bury their dead in above-ground tombs so that the coffins will not float to the surface during floods or heavy rains. These cemeteries are known as "cities of the dead" because they look like small cities. Their above-ground vaults and elaborate temples and mausoleums, trimmed with fancy ironwork and surrounded by fences, are connected by a network of sidewalks.

The oldest cemeteries in the city, St. Louis Cemetery No. 1 and St. Louis Cemetery No. 2, are located near the French Quarter. The tomb of the nineteenth-century voodoo queen, Marie Laveau, is in St. Louis Cemetery No. 1, and scenes from the movie *Interview with the*

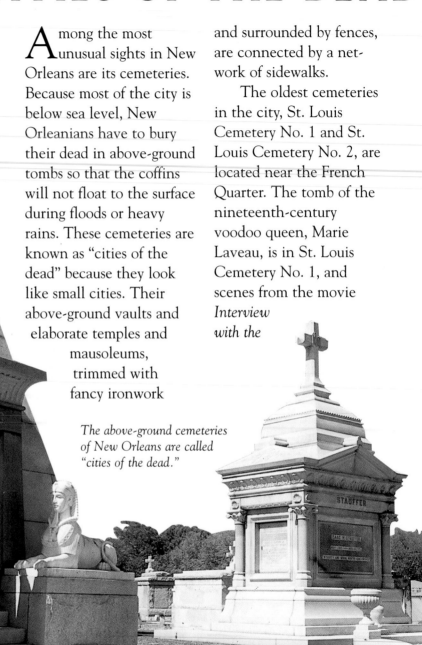

The above-ground cemeteries of New Orleans are called "cities of the dead."

Vampire were shot in the Garden District's Lafayette Cemetery. (The movie was based on a novel by New Orleans resident Anne Rice, who lives in the Garden District.) Each year on November 1, All Saints Day, many New Orleans families go to the cemeteries to pay their respects to departed family members. After they spruce up the tombs, they often eat picnic lunches and socialize with other families amid the tombs.

Nineteenth-century voodoo queen Marie Laveau

Voodoo

Voodoo is a religion that combines elements of African religions and Catholicism. Trances and magical practices play a part in voodoo rituals. There are an estimated 20,000 voodoo believers in New Orleans, and signs of voodoo practice can sometimes be seen in the city's cemeteries.

BIG MUDDY

Water still plays an important role in the daily life of New Orleans. The Mississippi River is the city's economic lifeline, but it presents a constant threat—floods. At New Orleans, the river flows 10 feet to 15 feet (3 meters to 4.5 meters) above sea level and carries hundreds of thousands of gallons of muddy water past the city. The mighty river is also at its widest and deepest at New Orleans: 2,220 feet (677 m) wide and 212 feet (65 m) deep. The city's ground elevation ranges from 5 feet (1.5 m) below sea level to 17 feet (5.2 m) above, and some parts of the city are sinking at a rate of 3 inches (7.6 centimeters) per century. Add to this the fact that the city gets about 62 inches (157.5 cm) of rainfall a year—more than

The New Orleans skyline at sunset from the Mississippi River

any other major U.S. city—and it's easy to see that there's a problem.

A flood in 1927 killed 500 people and led to the construction of a protective ring of large earth-and-concrete levees (dams) around the city. Seventeen pumping sta-

tions control water gates that divert floodwaters away from the city. These structures, along with more than 100 miles (161 kilometers) of canals, are the only barriers that prevent New Orleans from being underwater.

A stern-wheel paddleboat on the Mississippi River at New Orleans

THE RIVER

In February 1682, French explorer René-Robert Cavelier, Sieur de La Salle, boarded a canoe in what is now Ohio. Joined by fifty-six other Frenchmen, he traveled all the way down the Mississippi River, arriving at the Gulf of Mexico two months later. He claimed for France the entire Mississippi River and all of the lands drained by its tributaries. La Salle named the region Louisiana in honor of the French king, Louis XIV. France began establishing a colony in these lands and by 1712 had set up several small forts and villages on the shores of the Mississippi and along the Gulf of Mexico coastline.

René-Robert Cavelier, Sieur de La Salle
(REH-NAY-roe-BARE kah-voll-YAY, SYOOHR duh lah SAHL)

In 1717, colonial governor Jean Baptiste Le Moyne, Sieur de Bienville, received orders to establish a port city on the Mississippi. He selected a strip of land located between Lake Pontchartrain and a wide bend in the river. The site was nearly 110 miles (176 kilometers) upriver from the Gulf of Mexico.

Bienville decided to build the city at this spot because it was halfway between two important French forts. He also thought the site was far enough from the coast that it would be protected from high tides and hurricanes.

Others, including French engineers, thought that Bienville was crazy to build a city at the site. Bienville affectionately called the spot "the beautiful crescent in the river." In reality, it sat in the midst of a swamp teeming with snakes, alligators, and mosquitoes. The river was 200 feet (61 m) deep at the crescent, and its rushing

Jean Baptiste Le Moyne

waters didn't seem suitable for a busy port. The area's heavy rainfall would no doubt turn the town's roads into a muddy mess. The local Choctaw and Biloxi Indians had ignored the site for hundreds of years, choosing to build their villages in more favorable locations.

The early French colonists struggled to survive the hostile environment, and by 1721 New Orleans boasted many barracks, several houses, and a wooden storehouse. A hurricane that year wiped out most of the buildings,

New Orleans as it looked in 1719

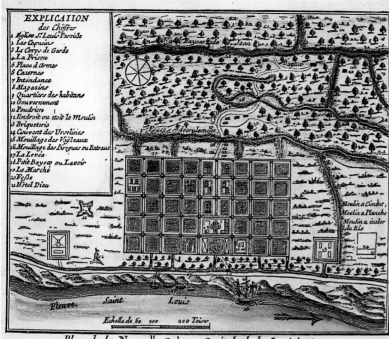

Plan de la Nouvelle Orleans Capitale de la Louisiane 1

however. The following spring, engineer Adrian de Pauger arrived from France to oversee the reconstruction of the city. He laid out the city's streets in a grid pattern. The residents, mostly traders, built sturdier houses of brick and wood. Despite the many hardships, they were determined to stay. New Orleans became the capital of Louisiana in 1723, and the French colony slowly established itself over the next forty years.

Adrian de Pauger laid out the streets of New Orleans in the grid pattern shown at left.

Namesake

Bienville named his new settlement Nouvelle Orléans in honor of Philippe II, duc D'Orléans (1674–1723). The uncle of France's child king Louis XV, Orléans served as the regent, or acting king, of France from 1715 until 1723, when Louis XV assumed power at age thirteen. When the United States purchased the Louisiana Territory from France, the name of Bienville's city was changed into English: New Orleans.

Jean Baptiste Le Moyne, Sieur de Bienville (ZHAN BOP-TEEST LUH MWAN, SYOOHR DUH B-YEN-VEEL)
Pontchartrain (PONT-CHER-TRAIN)
Nouvelle Orléans (NOO-VELL ORE-LAY-AWN)
Philippe II, duc D'Orleans (FEE-LEEP DOOH, DEWK DORE-LAY-AWN)
Adrian de Pauger (AY-DREE-AN DUH PAWG-ER)

THE SPANISH PERIOD

By 1762, it became clear that the mighty English army would gain control of the French colonies in Canada. France wanted to prevent its archenemy from seizing its other North American colonies, so by a secret treaty it gave New Orleans and all of the Louisiana colony west of the Mississippi River to Spain.

During the period of Spanish rule (1762–1800), the relationship between the residents of New Orleans and the governors sent by Spain to rule the colony were strained. The city's residents never adopted Spanish culture or customs, and French remained the language spoken. Today, about the only visible reminder of the Spanish period is found in the architecture of the French Quarter.

A Spanish-style New Orleans house with a private inner courtyard

Devastating fires burned the city to the ground in 1788 and 1794. After the second fire, the buildings that went up were made with sturdier materials and were built in the Spanish style, which featured private inner courtyards and elaborate wrought-iron balconies facing the street.

The facade of an early New Orleans house

A Pirate's Tale

One of the most colorful personalities in New Orleans's history, Jean Lafitte (1780?–1826?) led a band of pirates headquartered in the swamps south of the city. Lafitte's men robbed Spanish ships in the Gulf of Mexico and sold slaves. From his blacksmith shop on Bourbon Street (which still stands), Lafitte planned his crimes and sold his booty. When Governor William Claiborne offered $500 for Lafitte's capture in 1813, the pirate jokingly issued his own proclamation, offering $1,500 for the governor's capture. After Lafitte and his men helped the Americans defeat the British at the Battle of New Orleans, they were pardoned for their past crimes. No one knows exactly what happened to Lafitte after the war. Various legends contend that he returned to piracy, went to fight with South American revolutionary leader Simón Bolívar, or died of yellow fever.

AN AMERICAN CITY

In 1800, powerful French emperor Napoleon Bonaparte demanded that Spain return Louisiana to France. King Charles IV of Spain agreed on one condition: France had to promise never to give or sell the territory to any other nation. Napoleon agreed to this condition but soon ignored his pact with Spain. In April 1803, he sold the vast Louisiana Territory to the United States. On December 20, 1803, colonial officials lowered the French flag flying over the Place d'Armes in New Orleans and

The Louisiana Purchase papers were signed in the Cabildo (below), a building from which the Spanish once governed New Orleans.

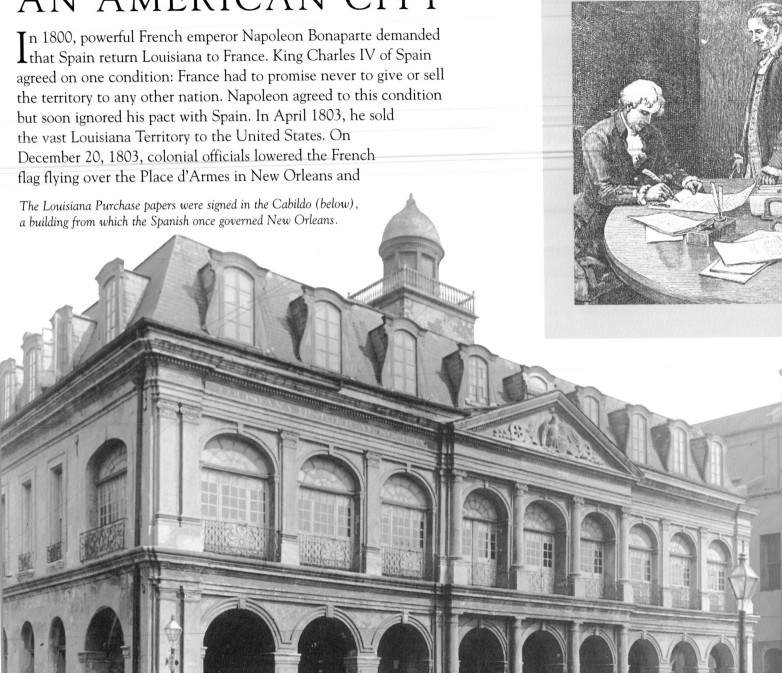

The Louisiana Purchase

Napoleon needed a great deal of money to pay for his wars in Europe and realized that his plans to build a French empire in Louisiana were unrealistic. At the same time, U.S. president Thomas Jefferson had his eye on New Orleans. He believed that the United States needed the port city in order to the develop its Western frontier. Not wanting the French colony to fall into the hands of England, Napoleon sold the entire Louisiana Territory, which included New Orleans, to the United States for about $15 million. Through the Louisiana Purchase, the United States doubled in size, gaining nearly 800,000 square miles (2 million sq km) of land.

raised the U.S. flag. After briefly being French again, the city's residents were now American.

When New Orleans became a U.S. city in 1803, it was a busy port with a population of nearly 10,000. It soon became the center of trade along the American Western frontier. Rice, sugar, tobacco, cotton, and other crops were the main goods that moved over its docks.

Most of the residents of New Orleans were French-speaking Catholics of French or Spanish descent. These Creoles, as they called themselves, felt that they had nothing in common with the Protestant, English-speaking Americans who now governed them. Canal Street, then the widest street in the United States, became the boundary between the Creoles, who lived in the French Quarter, and the growing number of Americans, who lived in the Faubourg St. Mary (now known as the Garden District).

On April 30, 1812, the Territory of Orleans became the state of Louisiana. Only seven weeks after Louisiana was admitted to the Union as the eighteenth state, the United States declared war on England. The British seized the upper hand early in the War of 1812. They even captured and ransacked Washington, D.C., in August 1814. From that point, however, the tide began to turn in favor of the American forces.

New Orleanians celebrate the Louisiana Purchase in the streets outside the Cabildo.

Napoleon Bonaparte (NUH-POLE-EE-UN BONE-UH-PART)
Place d'Armes (PLASS DARM)
Faubourg St. Mary (FOE-BERG SAINT MARE-EE)

THE BATTLE OF NEW ORLEANS

In December 1814, New Orleans prepared for a British attack. To defend the city, General Andrew Jackson recruited any local man who could handle a rifle. Choctaw Indians, sharpshooters from Kentucky and Tennessee, and free men of color (blacks who had never been slaves, had been freed by their masters, or had bought their freedom) also joined the general's forces. Jackson even convinced Jean Lafitte and his gang of pirates to fight for the United States by promising to get them pardoned for their past crimes.

Andrew Jackson at the Battle of New Orleans

Left:British general Edward Pakenham leading the attack on U.S. General Andrew Jackson during the Battle of New Orleans on January 8, 1815 Below: This statue of Andrew Jackson stands in Jackson Square.

Jackson set up his defenses at Chalmette, 6 miles (10 km) east of New Orleans. On January 8, 1815, British general Edward Pakenham launched an all-out attack on Jackson's 3,000 men. As the British troops advanced, Jackson's sharp-eyed riflemen, crouching behind cotton bales, methodically shot down the charging British. When the battle was over, more than 2,000 British soldiers, including Pakenham, lay dead or wounded. Only seven of Jackson's men died.

The victory gave New Orleanians a reason to be proud of their new country. Andrew Jackson, the hero of the Battle of New Orleans, would become the seventh U.S. president. Thirty years later, the Place d'Armes in New Orleans would be renamed Jackson Square in his honor.

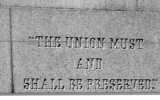

MAJOR GENERAL ANDREW JACKSON

"THE UNION MUST AND SHALL BE PRESERVED"

THE STEAMBOAT AGE

The *New Orleans*, the first steamboat to voyage the Mississippi River, arrived in New Orleans in January 1812. Much faster than other boats at the time, steamboats completely changed trade and travel on the Mississippi because they could go upriver as well as down. Crops from the Midwest bound for the East Coast, South America, and Europe passed through New Orleans, as did manufactured goods on their way to the Midwest. New Orleans soon became the most important port in the South. Steamboats, schooners, and other boats jammed its docks, and people of many nationalities

Right: Sugar plantation workers leaving the fields at twilight

The busy port of New Orleans as it looked in the nineteenth century

and races mingled in the city. As trade increased, other businesses—such as banks and insurance companies—multiplied.

Between 1820 and 1860, New Orleans enjoyed an economic boom. Slave labor, coupled with the inventions of the cotton gin (1793) and a new method of granulating sugar (1795), boosted the output of cotton and sugarcane plantations throughout the South. By 1860, 2 million bales of cotton were shipped through New Orleans each year.

Despite the prosperity, New Orleans still experienced some bad times. Epidemics of yellow fever regularly struck the city. Transmitted by a certain type of mosquito, yellow fever damages the liver, causing the skin of victims to turn yellow, and kills many who contract the disease. New Orleans's worst epidemic occurred in 1853, when yellow fever killed 10,000 residents.

Slave labor boosted the production of cotton plantations throughout the South.

A NATION DIVIDED

In 1860, New Orleans had a population of 168,000, making it the largest city in the South and the sixth largest in the United States. Its trade totaled $324 million a year. As the home of a classical opera, many theaters, and classical concerts, it was a sophisticated city with a large wealthy class.

After the 1860 election of Abraham Lincoln, who ran on an antislavery platform, it became apparent that Louisiana would join other Southern states in seceding from the Union. Many people in New Orleans were torn over the issue of secession. Although they opposed leaving the Union because they wanted to maintain their prosperity, they strongly supported slavery. In the end, most agreed with the Louisiana legislature's decision in 1861 to secede.

Right: Union captain David G. Farragut, who was in charge of a fleet of 44 ships that captured New Orleans during the Civil War
Below: The Confederate cruiser Sumter in 1861

When the Civil War began in April 1861, the Union navy quickly blockaded the mouth of the Mississippi River and most of the ports along the Gulf. The ships successfully cut off supplies to Confederate troops and civilians. On April 24, 1862, Union captain David Farragut and his fleet of 44 ships charged past Confederate defenses on the Mississippi River south of New Orleans. Knowing that he could not defend the city, Confederate general Mansfield Lovell withdrew his troops, and Union forces seized the city. New Orleans became an occupied city, and for the rest of the war, residents maintained a tense but mostly peaceful relationship with the Union army.

The Farragut fleet captured New Orleans on April 24, 1862.

REBUILDING A GREAT CITY

In 1867, with passage of the federal Reconstruction acts, African-Americans in New Orleans voted for the first time. During the Reconstruction era, many Northern businessmen flocked to the city hoping to make quick money. The city began the slow, difficult process of rebuilding itself. Despite occasional riots, labor unrest, and corruption in city government in the late nineteenth and early twentieth centuries, the people of New Orleans revived their city's economy. It became an important rail-

Left: St. Louis Cathedral and the Place d'Armes before restoration by the Vieux Carré Commission

The Vieux Carré

Many residents began worrying that the city's historical buildings were decaying and would be lost forever. In 1921, the Vieux Carré Commission was established and given the power to regulate architecture. The commission supervised the restoration of the old buildings in the French Quarter. St. Louis Cathedral, the Cabildo, Jackson Square, and the French Market were refurbished. (This restoration work continues today.)

road hub and reclaimed its lead as a shipping center. The major goods shipped through New Orleans included grain from the Midwest and bananas and coffee from Latin America. Timber and rice were big businesses, and the first oil well in Louisiana was erected in 1901. Oil refineries and various types of factories sprang up along the Mississippi from New Orleans upriver to Baton Rouge. As prosperity returned, mansions were built along the main roads, especially in the Garden District.

A mansion in the Garden District

Baton Rouge (BAT-un ROOZH)

A GROWING METROPOLIS

New Orleans grew in size as land was reclaimed by pumping water out of swamps. The city and its population spread out along the river. In 1961, construction of the amazing Pontchartrain Causeway was completed. The 24-mile- (39-km-) long bridge, the world's longest, allowed people working in the city to live in Covington and other towns on the opposite side of Lake Pontchartrain. New Orleans had become a city within a city, with old New Orleans in the center, surrounded by such suburbs as Arabi, Algiers, Gretna, Westwego, Jefferson, Harahan, Metairie, and Kenner. On September 9, 1965, Hurricane Betsy struck New Orleans, damaging many buildings and flooding many neighborhoods.

These residents of New Orleans had to be rescued from flood-waters caused by Hurricane Betsy.

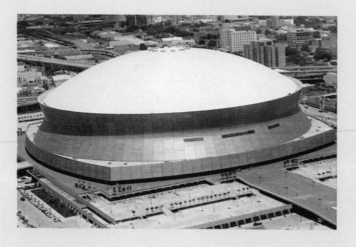

The World's Largest Room

When the vast indoor sports arena, the Superdome, opened in New Orleans in 1975, it was hailed as "a triumph of man's imagination." The titanic 27-story structure is so large that Houston's Astrodome could fit neatly inside it. In addition to serving as the home field of the NFL's Saints, the Superdome hosts rock concerts and a variety of sports events, including the annual Sugar Bowl football game.

In 1978, Ernest "Dutch" Morial became the first African-American elected mayor of New Orleans. During his eight years in office, Morial made improvements to the city's docks and supported the construction of a new convention center to attract events to the city. His son, Marc Morial, was elected mayor in 1994 at age thirty-six. He took charge of a city hampered by the social problems that plague many large U.S. cities, but he promised to make New Orleans a better and safer city.

*New Orleans mayor
Ernest "Dutch" Morial*

New Orleans has an international reputation for its music. It is the hometown of many acclaimed musicians, including Ferdinand "Jelly Roll" Morton, Louis Prima, Mahalia Jackson, Fats Domino, Randy Newman, the Marsalis family, the Neville Brothers, and, above all, Louis Armstrong. It's no coincidence that New Orleans has produced so many musicians. Name almost any type of music—jazz, pop, rock, reggae, soul, blues, funk, Cajun, zydeco, gospel, country and western, alternative, rap, or classical—and you'll find someone playing it somewhere in the city. From its clubs and symphony halls to the streets of the French Quarter, New Orleans pulsates with music.

ALL THAT JAZZ

Legend has it that jazz was born in New Orleans, traveled up the Mississippi River to Chicago, made its way east to New York City, and then spread to the rest of the world. This is basically true, but it's not the whole story. Music scholars have traced the origins of jazz to many different places. Jazz has its roots in Africa. Beginning in the seventeenth century, West Africans were captured and transported across the Atlantic Ocean to the Americas to be sold as slaves. They brought their rich cultural traditions with them, including music. In the American South, African-American music expanded to include spirituals and work songs. Over time, this music absorbed traditions from many other types of music, including blues, ragtime, military marches, and European folk music. This completely new type of music was jazz.

Although it is not really the birthplace of jazz, New Orleans has played an important role in the history of jazz. In the early 1800s, the city set aside an empty lot called Congo Square, where free and enslaved blacks were permitted to sing, dance, and play their drums and other homemade instruments.

Musicians in Congo Square (now called Beauregard Square)

46

Congo Square, now called Beauregard Square, is the site of the Morris F. X. Jeff Auditorium in Louis Armstrong Park. By the late nineteenth century, African-American bands had become a vibrant part of the cultural life of New Orleans. Dozens of black social clubs and civic organizations boasted their own brass bands.

New Orleans soon became a good place for musicians, particularly African-Americans, to make a living. The bustling port had many nightspots that needed musicians to entertain their customers. One section of the city, called Storyville, became notorious for its honky-tonks, dance halls, and gambling houses in which music could be heard. Many people considered this new music disreputable because it was associated with the unsavory nightlife of New Orleans. At the same time, blues, ragtime, and band music—other musical traditions that contributed to the birth of jazz—were developing in other regions of the United States.

The Jazz Funeral

The jazz funeral is a custom unique to New Orleans. It originated in the late nineteenth century. When a member of an African-American social club died, the club's band led the funeral march. The musicians played a slow-paced song, known as a dirge, on the way to the cemetery. After the burial, the band marched from the cemetery, and the drummers began playing a more upbeat tempo. A block or two away from the cemetery, the band would launch into a quick-step march. Bystanders often joined in, creating what is known as the second line. "When the Saints Go Marching In" became the most popular post-funeral song. Today, jazz funerals are rare, reserved mostly for musicians.

This completely new kind of music found its permanent name in 1917. The Original Dixieland Jazz Band, an all-white group, became an overnight sensation playing the kind of music that African-American musicians had been playing for years. As the home to such early jazz giants as Jelly Roll Morton, Joe "King" Oliver, and Louis Armstrong, New Orleans soon emerged as the center of jazz. Jazz has since gone through many changes—including such styles as bebop, cool, and fusion—and spread throughout the world.

As jazz quickly spread across the United States and the world, New Orleans could no longer brag that it was the center of the jazz universe. But such local favorites as Professor Longhair and Pete Fountain kept the music playing, and jazz lives on in the city.

There are many places where jazz is played, but the most famous is Preservation Hall. Opened in the 1960s, Preservation Hall re-creates the old New Orleans music hall and gives old-time legends a regular place to play.

Left: Pete Fountain, playing a solo clarinet

Below: Members of the Original Dixieland Jazz Band, left to right: Eddie Edwards (trombone), Nick La Rocca (trumpet), Tony Spargo (drums), Henry Ragas (piano), and Larry Shields (clarinet)

Louis Armstrong

One of the twentieth century's most beloved and influential musicians, Louis Armstrong was born in New Orleans on August 4, 1901. Raised by his mother and grandmother, he grew up in the poorest, roughest neighborhood in the city. Armstrong quit school after the third grade because he had to get a job to help support his family. At age thirteen, he was arrested for firing a pistol loaded with blanks during a Fourth of July celebration. Armstrong was sent to a juvenile detention center. There, he received his first music lessons and his first horn, a cornet.

A year later, Armstrong was released. He worked at several low-paying jobs and kept practicing his horn. Bandleader Joe Oliver took the young musician under his wing, and before he was twenty, Armstrong was playing the trumpet so well that he astonished local musicians. In 1925, he formed his own band, the Hot Five, which created a fresh, new sound that changed jazz forever. Armstrong's colossal talent and dynamic personality made him a larger-than-life superstar. Sporting the nicknames Satchmo (short for Satchel Mouth) and later Pops, he became the symbol and goodwill ambassador of traditional jazz. Satchmo traveled the world, performing before adoring crowds until his death in 1971.

Every night, jazz fans from around the world line up outside the hall, awaiting their turn to listen to a set or two.

The city continues to produce many superb jazz musicians, most notably the Marsalis family—pianist Ellis, trumpeter Wynton, saxophonist Branford, trombonist Delfaeyo, and drummer Jason—and singer Harry Connick Jr. Tulane University has an impressive collection of jazz information, and fascinating displays at the Jazz Museum in the old U.S. Mint building trace jazz from its origins to the present.

A 1940 photograph of jazz musician Jelly Roll Morton

THE MUSIC SCENE

Jazz isn't the only music heard in town. Almost every type of music pours out of the clubs throughout the French Quarter. Such local favorites as Dr. John, the Neville Brothers (Aaron, Art, Charles, and Cyril), Li'l Queenie, Marva Wright, and Allen Toussaint often perform at various places throughout the city. Traditional Cajun music, which features the accordion and fiddle, and zydeco—a combination of Cajun, rock, and country—are also very popular. The latest rock, rap, and soul can be heard throughout the city.

Classical music also has a home in the city. New Orleans was the first North American city to have a permanent opera company. Today, opera lovers flock to performances at the Theater of the Performing Arts. The Crescent City is also the home of the Louisiana Philharmonic Orchestra, which performs at the Pontchartrain Center and the Orpheum Theater.

A band playing Cajun music at Mulate's Cajun Restaurant in New Orleans

Often, the best place to hear music in New Orleans is on the streets. Unlike performers in other U.S. cities, musicians may legally perform on the streets for donations. The French Quarter is a popular place for musicians to play, hoping that passersby will drop some change into their hats or that the manager of one of the city's clubs will offer them a gig. Visitors are often surprised by the talents of the saxophonists, singers, accordionists, and other musicians standing on street corners giving it their all.

Street musicians (left and right) performing in the French Quarter

Despite its nineteenth-century ambiance and leisurely pace, New Orleans experiences many of the problems of other large cities. Traffic chokes its main roads. Poverty, unemployment, and crime plague many of its neighborhoods. New Orleans has one of the highest murder rates in the United States, and its population is slowly declining as residents move to the suburbs or to other cities. Many sectors of the city's economy, however, remain strong. The tourism industry continues to grow, and about 10 million people visit New Orleans each year. In addition to the city's many tourist attractions, events at the Convention Center and Superdome help keep visitors' dollars pouring into the city.

A CELEBRATION OF DIVERSITY

Although it has its share of troubles, New Orleans remains a city of remarkable diversity, shaped by the customs and traditions of many nations. Immigrants of French, African, Spanish, Irish, Italian, German, and Latin American descent have all played a part in creating the unique character of New Orleans.

African-Americans make up about 62 percent of the city's population. The first Africans arrived in New Orleans in 1720. They numbered 500 and were sold into slavery. In spite of their dire situation, Africans and their descendants created a strong cultural bond and played an important role in building New Orleans.

Italians have also played a large role in building New Orleans. New Orleans was a popular destination for Italian immigrants, and by 1850, the city boasted the largest Italian community in the United States. Many Italians settled in the French Quarter, which became known as Little Italy during the late nineteenth century. Currently, about one-sixth of New Orleans's population has an Italian heritage.

New Orleans has always had a sizable Irish population. Irish mercenaries serving in the French army were stationed in New Orleans when it was a French city. By the outbreak of the Civil War, people of Irish descent numbered about 25,000. Irish workers were later recruited to dig the city's canals, and many lived in a neighborhood known as the Irish Channel.

Many other national and ethnic groups make up the population of New Orleans, including German, Asian, Latin American, and Caribbean. For example, about 120,000 Hondurans live in the city. The Hondurans came to New Orleans to work for the large fruit companies in the 1960s, and today they represent the largest Honduran community in the United States.

Artist Richard C. Thomas works on a painting at his New Orleans gallery.

Adopting the spirit of New Orleans, all of these groups celebrate their cultural heritage by hosting festivals and colorful parades. The African-American community observes its rich history in such events as the week-long Black Heritage Festival. The highlight of the Irish community's year is the annual St. Patrick's Day (March 17) celebration. The parades feature marchers decked out in traditional green, and there are a few floats. Imitating Mardi Gras parades, the riders throw carrots and cabbages—traditional Irish vegetables—into the crowds. Two days later, the Italian community throws its own festive parade to celebrate St. Joseph's Day.

New Orleans has transformed itself from a remote French outpost in the middle of a swamp to a great modern city. Bienville's "beautiful crescent in the river" has survived floods, hurricanes, epidemics, slavery, war, hard times, and decay, and today it bustles with life, diversity, and originality. As New Orleanians look to the future, they hope to continue making progress without destroying the city's unique character—all the while letting the good times roll.

Left: A street performer in Jackson Square wraps a child in balloons.

Right: Colorful toys like these are thrown to children during parades.

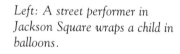

FAMOUS LANDMARKS

The Old Mint Building

Jackson Square

French Quarter
The oldest part of New Orleans. The narrow streets of this 86-block National Historic District has charming nineteenth-century buildings, town houses, and cottages—many adorned with fancy ironwork.

Jackson Square
Established in 1721 as a field for military drills. Today, it is a pedestrian mall—usually bustling with townsfolk, tourists, and street performers—that surrounds a small park.

St. Louis Cathedral
The oldest active cathedral in the United States (opened 1794), this small, white-stone church features pastel-colored ceiling frescoes and a large mural depicting Louis IX of France announcing the Seventh Crusade.

French Market
One of the oldest public markets in the United States, it is now a five-block complex of cafes, shops, and historic buildings.

Old Ursuline Convent
The oldest building in New Orleans (built 1752), it survived the eighteenth-century fires. It was the first convent in Louisiana and is located on Chartres Street in the French Quarter.

Cabildo
Reopened in 1994, this historic building was originally the headquarters for the Spanish governing council. The Louisiana Purchase papers were signed there in 1803. It is now home to the Louisiana State Museum.

Old Mint Building
From 1838 to 1910, it housed a U.S. mint, which minted tons of coins—as much as $5 million per month. It is now home to a jazz museum and Mardi Gras exhibits.

Beauregarde-Keyes House
Built in 1826, this Greek Revival house has lovely English gardens and a museum that features personal effects of its two former residents, Confederate general Pierre Beauregarde and regional writer Frances Parkinson Keyes.

The New Orleans Museum of Art

The Cabildo

The courtyard of the
Beauregard-Keyes House

Confederate Memorial Museum
The oldest museum (opened 1891) in Louisiana, it is full of relics, documents, paintings, and weapons from the U.S. Civil War, including the personal effects of Confederate president Jefferson Davis.

New Orleans Fair Grounds
Located in the Central Business District, it is the home of the Fair Ground's Racetrack, the nation's third-oldest horse racing track (built 1872), and is the main site of the Jazz and Heritage Festival.

Audubon Park
A 400-acre (162-hectare) park in the Garden District known for its stately, Spanish-moss-draped live oak trees. It is also home to the Audubon Zoo.

Louis Armstrong Park
Named after the hometown jazz great, this park is situated on the original site of Congo Square and is now home to many festivals and celebrations. It is the site of the municipal auditorium, which hosts operas, plays, and Mardi Gras balls.

Preservation Hall
Opened in the 1960s, this performance space recalls old-time New Orleans music halls. Jazz fans from around the world flock to it to hear traditional jazz.

Louisiana Superdome
Opened in 1975, this indoor arena has been called the world's largest room. It covers 9.7 acres (3.9 ha), rises 27 stories high, and seats more than 73,000.

Ernest N. Morial Convention Center
Originally housing the Louisiana Exhibit of the 1984 World's Fair, this large hall opened as a convention center in 1985. With 750,000 square feet (69,675 sq m) of floor space, it is one of the largest convention centers in the world.

New Orleans Museum of Art (NOMA)
Located in City Park, NOMA is one of the nation's finest art museums. It has a permanent collection of 35,000 objects and features special collections of Degas paintings and Fabergé eggs.

FAST FACTS

POPULATION

City: 485,000
Metropolitan Area: 1,300,000

LOCATION New Orleans is located in southeastern Louisiana between the Mississippi River and Lake Pontchartrain. It is 107 miles (172 km) from the Gulf of Mexico.

CLIMATE New Orleans has a subtropical climate—hot and very humid. Frequent and sometimes heavy rain is typical. In winter, occasional large and sudden drops in temperature occur, but these cold spells are not prolonged. January temperatures average 52 degrees Fahrenheit (11° Celsius). In July, the average temperature is 83 degrees Fahrenheit (28° Celsius).

ECONOMY One of the largest and most important cities in the southern United States, New Orleans is a major international port and a regional center of business and banking. Imported products include coffee and bananas, and its exports include oil, chemicals, cotton, and grains. Food processing, oil, aerospace, chemical products, and tourism are its major industries.

CHRONOLOGY

1682
La Salle claims for France the Mississippi River and all of the lands drained by its tributaries.

1717
Bienville selects the site for New Orleans.

1721
A hurricane wipes out most of the city's buildings.

1723
New Orleans is named the capital of the colony of Louisiana.

1762
By treaty, France gives New Orleans to Spain.

1794
The first services are held at St. Louis Cathedral.

1800
Spain returns New Orleans to France.

1803
The United States buys the Louisiana Territory from France in the Louisiana Purchase; New Orleans becomes a U.S. city.

1812
Louisiana becomes the eighteenth state; the first steamboat to voyage the Mississippi arrives in New Orleans; the War of 1812 begins.

1815
U.S. forces led by Andrew Jackson rout the British in the Battle of New Orleans.

1820–60
New Orleans enjoys an economic boom based on cotton and sugar; the Mystick Krewe of Comus is founded in 1857.

1861
Louisiana secedes from the Union.

1862
Union forces seize and occupy New Orleans.

1867
The city's African-American residents vote for the first time.

1877
Federal troops leave New Orleans as the Reconstruction era ends.

1884
Tulane University is founded.

The gardens of Longue Vue House, a beautiful planta-tion near West End Park

1891
The Confederate Memorial Museum opens.

1901
Louis Armstrong is born in New Orleans.

1917
A New Orleans band, the Original Dixieland Jazz Band, becomes a sensation, giving jazz its name.

1921
The Vieux Carré Commission is established; restoration of the French Quarter begins.

1935
Bonnet Carré Spillway, designed to divert floodwaters into Lake Pontchartrain, is completed.

1950s
The population of the city expands into the suburbs of Jefferson Parish.

1960
City schools begin to integrate.

1961
Construction of the Pontchartrain Bridge is completed.

1965
Hurricane Betsy strikes, flooding much of the city.

1975
The Louisiana Superdome opens; restoration of the French Market is completed.

1978
Ernest "Dutch" Morial is elected the city's first African-American mayor.

1984
New Orleans hosts the 1984 Louisiana World Exposition (World's Fair).

1986
The Superdome hosts Super Bowl XX.

1987
Pope John Paul II celebrates a Papal Mass in New Orleans.

1994
The Cabildo reopens after being damaged by fire in 1988; Marc Morial is elected mayor.

1997
The Superdome hosts Super Bowl XXXI.

1998
Marc Morial reelected mayor.

NEW ORLEANS

A B C D E F G H I J K

1 2 3 4 5 6 7

Louisiana Superdome

CIVIC CENTER

Canal Street

St. Louis Cemetery No. 2

STORYVILLE

Louis Armstrong Park

Theater of the Performing Arts

Morris F.X. Jeff Auditorium

Congo Square

St. Louis Cemetery No. 1

Orpheum Theater

CENTRAL BUSINESS DISTRICT

Arnaud's

Broussard's

Bourbon Street

Antoine's

FRENCH QUARTER

Preservation Hall

Lafitte Blacksmith Shop

Number One Shell Square

St. Charles Street

Cabildo

St. Louis Cathedral

Beauregarde-Keyes House

Decatur Street

Jackson Square

Old Ursuline Convent

French Market

Moonwalk

Jazz Museum and Old U.S. Mint

North Peters Street

Confederate Memorial Museum

WAREHOUSE DISTRICT

Spanish Plaza

Mississippi River

Ernest N. Morial Convention Center

Riverwalk

ALGIERS

Algiers	H7	Cabildo	G4	Decatur Street	5 E-J	Jazz Museum	I5
Antoine's	G4	Canal Street	E 1-6	Ernest N. Morial	C,D 7	Kenner	L 2-3
Arabi	O3	Central Business	B,C 3	Convention Center		Lafayette Cemetery	N4
Arnaud's	F3	District		French Market	H5	Lafitte Blacksmith Shop	H3
Audubon Park	M3	Chalmette	O3	French Quarter	E-I 3-5	Lake Pontchartrain	L-O 1-2
Audubon Zoo	M3	City Park	N2	Garden District	N3	Longue Vue House	N2
Beauregarde-Keyes House	I4	Civic Center	C,D 2	Gretna	N,O 4	Louis Armstrong	G,H 1,2
Bourbon Street	E-G 3	Confederate Museum	B5	Harahan	L,M 3	Park	
Broussard's	F3	Congo Square	G2	Jackson Square	G 4-5	Louisiana Superdome	A,B 1,2

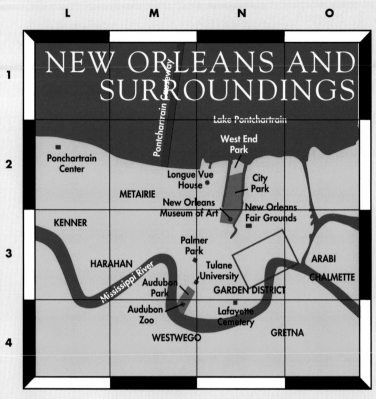

NEW ORLEANS AND SURROUNDINGS

L   M   N   O

1

Ponchartrain Expressway
Lake Pontchartrain

West End Park

2 Ponchartrain Center
Longue Vue House
City Park
METAIRIE
New Orleans Museum of Art
New Orleans Fair Grounds

KENNER

3 HARAHAN
Mississippi River
Palmer Park
Audubon Park
Tulane University
GARDEN DISTRICT
ARABI
CHALMETTE

4 Audubon Zoo
Lafayette Cemetery
WESTWEGO
GRETNA

Metairie	M2	Preservation Hall	G4
Mississippi River	E-K 5-7	Riverwalk	D7
Moonwalk	F-H 5	Spanish Plaza	E6
Morris F. X. Jeff	G2	St. Charles Street	A-K 4,5
Auditorium		St. Louis Cathedral	G4
New Orleans	N3	St. Louis Cemetery No. 1	F2
Fair Grounds		St. Louis Cemetery No. 2	F1
New Orleans	N2	Storyville	E,F 1,2
Museum of Art		Theater of the	H2
North Peters Street	H-K 4-7	Performing Arts	
Number One Shell Square	D4	Tulane University	M3
Old Ursuline Convent	I4	U.S. Mint Building	I5
Orpheum Theater	E3	Warehouse District	C,D 6
Palmer Park	M3	West End Park	N2
Pontchartrain Causeway	M1,2	Westwego	M4
Ponchartrain Center	L2		

GLOSSARY

ambiance: The feeling or mood of a particular place

bayou: A stream that flows slowly through a swamp or marsh

crawfish: A kind of shellfish that lives in fresh water and is used as food

cuisine: A style of cooking

epidemic: An outbreak of disease that makes many people in an area sick at the same time

flamboyant: Very elaborate or richly colored

gig: Musicians' slang for a job

mausoleum: A large above-ground tomb

mercenaries: Soldiers hired to serve a foreign country

penance: Prayers said or actions taken by sinners to atone for their sins

ragtime: A type of music popular in the early twentieth century

Reconstruction: The period following the Civil War when the Southern states reformed their governments

secede: To withdraw from a group or organization

spirituals: Religious songs

Picture Identifications

Cover: Riverside, accordionist at the Jazz and Heritage Festival, a Mardi Gras mask
Page 1: Mardi Gras souvenir masks for sale in the French Market
Pages 4–5: A float in a Mardi Gras parade
Page 5: A Mardi Gras figure
Pages 12–13: St. Louis Cathedral and Jackson Square
Pages 26–27: A painting of La Salle taking possession of Louisiana
Pages 44–45: The front line of the Treme Brass Band parading through the crowds at the New Orleans Jazz and Heritage Festival
Pages 52–53: Fireworks over the water alongside the Central Business District (CBD) of New Orleans

Photo Credits ©:

DDB Stock Photo — D. Donne Bryant, cover (background and front left), 10 (right), 17 (left), 23 (bottom), 25, 51 (right), 56 (background)
Karen Kohn & Associates, Ltd. — Cover (front right), 3, 5, 6 (left), 8 (top), 9 (right), 10 (left), 11 (top right), 15 (top), 17 (right), 18, 20 (pralines), 55 (top and bottom right), 60, 61
New England Stock Photo — Jeff Greenberg, 1; Jim Schwabel, 55 (left)
SuperStock International, Inc. — 4–5, 49; Ping Amranand, 52–53
Tony Stone Images, Inc. — Bob Thomason, 6 (right); Frank Siteman, 7; Michael Townsend, 14; Penny Tweedie, 15 (bottom); Don Smetzer, 23 (top)
H. Armstrong Roberts — W. Bertsch, 8 (bottom); F. Gordon, 16 (bottom), 57 (top), 59; J. Blank, 41
The Viesti Collection, Inc. — Richard Pasley, 9 (left), 11 (top left and bottom), 44–45
Cameramann International, Ltd. — 12–13, 35 (bottom)
International Stock — Andre Jenny, 16 (top), 22–23, 51 (left); Frank Grant, 19 (bottom right)
Photo Edit — Phil Borden, 19 (top); Bonnie Kamin, 21 (right), 50, 54; Dennis MacDonald, 40 (bottom); Leslye Borden, 47
Root Resources — Garry D. McMichael, 19 (bottom left)
Robert Holmes — 20–21, 46, 56 (inset), 57 (bottom left and right)
First Image West, Inc. — Tom Neiman, 24–25
Corbis-Bettmann — 26–27, 29 (bottom), 30, 31 (left), 32 (top), 33; Grant Smith, 32 (bottom); UPI, 43; Frank Driggs, 48 (right), 49 (bottom)
Stock Montage, Inc. — 28 (both pictures), 29 (top), 34, 36–37, 39
North Wind Picture Archives — 31 (right), 40 (top)
North Wind Pictures — 35 (top), 36 (top), 37, 38 (left)
AP/Wide World Photos — 38 (right), 42 (both pictures), 48 (left)

INDEX

Page numbers in boldface type indicate illustrations

Armstrong, Louis, 45, 48, 49, **49,** 59

Audubon Zoo, 5, 17, **17,** 57

Beauregarde, Pierre, 56

Beauregarde-Keyes House, 56, **57**

Beauregard Square (Congo Square), 46–47, **46**

Bienville, Jean Baptiste Le Moyne, Sieur de, 28, **28,** 29, 58

Biloxi Indians, 28

Bonaparte, Napoleon, 32, 33

Bonnet Carré Spillway, 59

Bourbon Street, 31

Cabildo, 15, **32,** 40, 56, **57,** 59

Cajuns, 5, 11, 18, 50, **50**

Canal Street, 33

Carnival, 6–9

Carollton, (neighborhood), 17

cemeteries, 22–23, **22, 23**

Central Business District, 16, **52–53,** 57

Charles IV, 32

chefs, 18, **19**

Choctaw Indians, 28, 34

Civic Center, 16

Civil War, 38–39, **38, 39,** 54, 57, 58

climate, 13, 58

Congo Square (Beauregard Square), 46–47, **46,** 57

Creoles, 18, 33

crime, 53

cultural heritage, 11, 13, 14, 30, 36, 46, 54–55

economy, 33, 36–37, 38, 40–41, 53, 58

Ernest Morial Convention Center, 16, 53, 57

ethnic festivals, 10, 55

ethnic people, 10, 11, 13, 54–55, **54**

Faubourg Marigny (neighborhood), 17

Faubourg St. Mary, **33**

foods, 5, 10, 15, **15,** 18–20, **18, 19, 20**

French Market, 15, **15,** 16, **20,** 40, 56, 59

French Quarter, 14, **14,** 16, 18, 22, 30, 33, 40, 45, 50, 51, **51,** 54, 56, 59

Garden District, 16, **16,** 17, 23, 33, 41, **41,** 57

Gentilly (neighborhood), 17

Gulf of Mexico, 27, 28, 39, 58

history, 27–43, 58–59

Hurricane Betsy, 42, **42–43,** 59

Jackson, Andrew, 15, 34–35, **34, 35,** 58

Jackson Square, **12–13,** 14, **14,** 15, 35, **35,** 40, **40,** 56, **56,** 62

Jazz and Heritage Festival, **cover,** 5, 10, **10, 11, 44–45,** 57

jazz funeral, 47, **47**

Jefferson, Thomas, 33

John Paul II, 59

Lafitte, Jean, 31, 34

Lake Pontchartrain, 28, 42, 58, 59

Lakeview (neighborhood), 17

La Salle, René-Robert Cavelier, Sieur de, **26–27,** 27, 58

Laveau, Marie, 22, **23**

Longue Vue House, **59**

Louis Armstrong, Park, 47, 57

Louis IX, 56

Louis XIV, 27

Louis XV, 29

Louisiana Philharmonic Orchestra, 50

Louisiana Purchase, 29, 32–33, **32, 33,** 56, 58

Louisiana Superdome, 16, 42, **42,** 53, 57, 59

Louisiana World's Fair, 57, 59

Mardi Gras, **cover, 1, 4–5,** 5, 6–9, **6, 7, 8, 9, 10, 11,** 55, 56, 57

Mardi Gras Indians, 9, **9,** 10

Mississippi River, 5, 24–25, **24, 25,** 27, 28, 36, 39, 46, 58

Morial, Ernest, 43, **43,** 59

Morial, Marc, 43, 59

Morton, Ferdinand "Jelly Roll," 45, 48, **49**

museums, 15, 49, 56, **56,** 57, **57,** 59

music, 7, 9, 10, **11, 44–45,** 45–51, **46, 47, 48, 49,** 50, **50, 51,** 57

New Orleans, Battle of, 31, 34–35, **34, 35,** 58

Old Mint Building, 49, 56, **56**

Old Ursuline Convent, 56

Oliver, Joe "King," 48, 49

Original Dixieland Jazz Band, 48, **48,** 59

Orpheum Theater, 50

Pakenham, General Edward, 35, **35**

Pauger, Adrian de, 29

Philippe II, 29

Place d'Armes, 32, 35, **40**

plantations, **36,** 37, **37**

Pontchartrain Causeway, 42

Pontchartrain Center, 50

population, 14, 33, 38, 54, 58

Preservation Hall, 48, 57

Reconstruction, 40, 58

restaurants, 17, 18, **19, 50**

Riverside, **cover,** 5

Riverwalk, 16

St. Louis Cathedral, 12–13, **14,** 15, 40, **40,** 56, **56,** 58

Spanish period, 15, 30–31, **30, 31,** 56

sports, 5, 42, 57

statehood, 33

steamboats, 5, **25,** 36–37, 58

Storyville, 47

streetcars, 16, **16**

street performers, 14–15, 51, **51, 55,** 56

Territory of Orleans, 33

Theater of the Performing Arts, 50

Tulane University, 49, 58

Vieux Carré, 14, **14,** 40, **40**

Vieux Carré Commission, 40, 59

voodoo, 23

Warehouse District, 17

War of 1812, 33–35, **34, 35,** 58

TO FIND OUT MORE

BOOKS

Coil, Suzanne M. *Mardi Gras!* New York: Macmillan, 1994.

Collier, James Lincoln. *Jazz: An American Saga*. New York: Henry Holt & Company, Inc., 1997.

Ellis, Veronica Freeman. *Wynton Marsalis*. Contemporary Biographies series. Austin, Texas: Raintree Steck-Vaughn, 1997.

Fodor's '98 New Orleans. New York: Fodor's Travel Publications, 1997.

Kent, Deborah. *Louisiana*. America the Beautiful series. Chicago: Childrens Press, 1991.

Hintz, Martin. *Destination New Orleans*. Port Cities of North America series. Minneapolis: Lerner Publications Company, 1997.

Hoyt-Goldsmith, Diane. *Mardi Gras: A Cajun Country Celebration*. New York: Holiday House, 1995.

King, David C. and V. A. Koeth. *New Orleans*. Battlefields Across America series. Brookfield, Conn.: Millbrook Press, 1998.

Marsh, Carole. *Louisiana Kids' Cookbook*. Atlanta: Gallopade, 1994.

Medearis, Angela Shelf. *Little Louis and the Jazz Band: The Story of Louis "Satchmo" Armstrong*. New York: Lodestar, 1994.

Sakurai, Gail. *The Louisiana Purchase*. Cornerstones of Freedom series. Danbury, Conn.: Children's Press, 1998.

Smith, Michael P. and Allison Miner. *Jazz Fest Memories*. Gretna, Louisiana: Pelican, 1997.

Talent, Robert. *The Pirate Lafitte and the Battle of New Orleans*. Gretna, Louisiana: Pelican Publishing Company, 1993.

Vogt, Lloyd. *A Young Person's Guide to New Orleans Houses*. Gretna, Louisiana: Pelican Pusblishing Company, 1992.

ONLINE SITES

New Orleans Online
http://neworleansonline.com/
A really good site aimed mostly at tourists but chock-full of useful information on history, interesting New Orleans characters, and special places in the city.

New Orleans Metropolitan Convention and Visitors Bureau
http://www.nawlins.com/
Check out the visitor's guide and get up-to-date facts, news, and information on future events.

Cityview
http://cityview.com/neworleans/
A comprehensive site that provides information on things to do in New Orleans and a schedule of events.

Mardi G. Raccoon
http://www.mardi.com/
Mardi G. Raccoon provides information for young people on cool places and activities in New Orleans.

Audubon Zoo
http://www.auduboninstitute.org/html/aa_zoomain.html
Enjoy this colorful site, which includes a quick tour, a creature feature, and a section on new adventures in the zoo.

New Orleans Museum of Art
http://www.noma.org/
Explore the online gallery and get information on the museum's permanent collection and special exhibitions.

Louisiana Superdome
http://www.superdome.com/
Take a virtual tour of the building, find out interesting facts, and get information on coming events.

The Gumbo Pages
http://www.gumbopages.com/
Provides information on Cajun music, food, and culture in New Orleans.

Jazz Archive
http://www.tulane.edu/~lmiller/JazzHome.html
Find out what's going on at Tulane University's William Ransom Hogan Archive of New Orleans Jazz.

ABOUT THE AUTHOR

G. S. Prentzas is a book editor who works in New York City. He is the author of seven nonfiction books for young readers, including a biography of Thurgood Marshall and an ethnography of the Kwakiutl Indians. He enjoys traveling, camping, and photography. New Orleans is one of his favorite U.S. cities.